Things Will NEVER Be the Same

written and illustrated by

Tomie dePaola

A 26 FAIRMOUNT AVENUE BOOK

G. P. Putnam's Sons • New York

Book designed by Gina DiMassi. Text set in Garth Graphic.
Library of Congress Cataloging-in-Publication Data
De Paola, Tomie. Things will never be the same / written and illustrated
by Tomie dePaola. p. cm. — (A 26 Fairmount Avenue book)
Summary: Author-illustrator Tomie De Paola describes his experiences
at home and in school in 1941 when he was a boy. 1. De Paola, Tomie—Childhood and
youth—Juvenile literature. 2. De Paola, Tomie—Homes and haunts—Connecticut—
Meriden—Juvenile literature. 3. Authors, American—20th century—Biography—
Juvenile literature. 4. Meriden (Conn.)—Biography—Juvenile literature.
[1. De Paola, Tomie—Childhood and youth. 2. Authors, American. 3. Illustrators.]
I. Title. PS3554.E11474 Z478 2003 813'.54—dc21 2002005995
ISBN 0-399-23982-0
1 3 5 7 9 10 8 6 4 2
First Impression

For my first best friend,
Jean Houdlette Turco,
and my first girlfriend,
Jean Minor Kenny—
and, of course,
Bob Hechtel, and Mario.

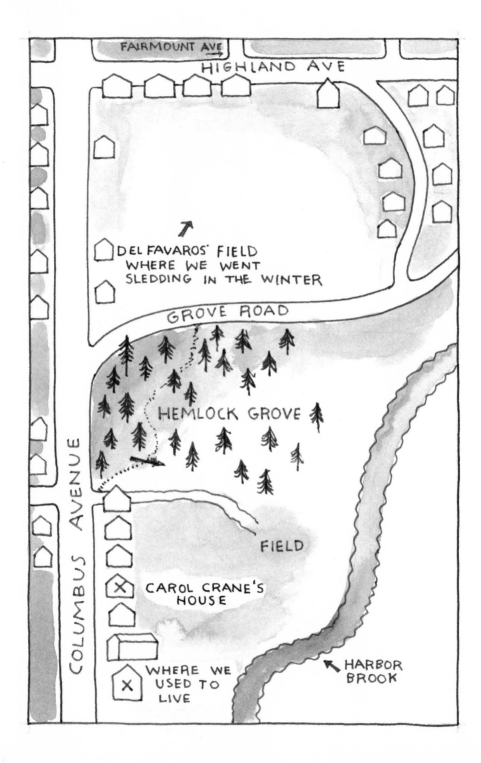

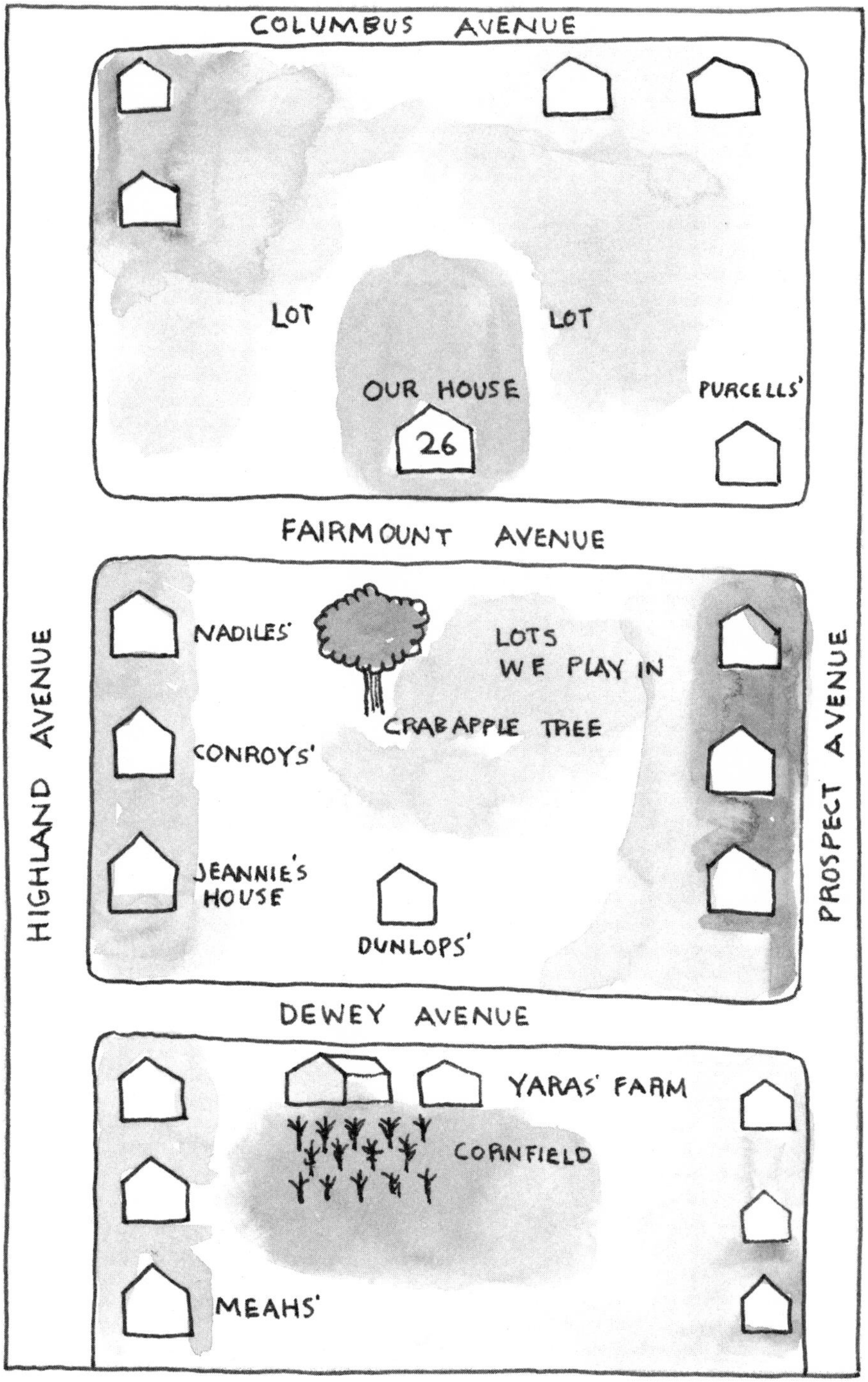
COLUMBUS AVENUE
LOT
LOT
OUR HOUSE
26
PURCELLS'
FAIRMOUNT AVENUE
NADILES'
LOTS WE PLAY IN
CRABAPPLE TREE
CONROYS'
JEANNIE'S HOUSE
DUNLOPS'
HIGHLAND AVENUE
PROSPECT AVENUE
DEWEY AVENUE
YARAS' FARM
CORNFIELD
MEAHS'

Chapter One

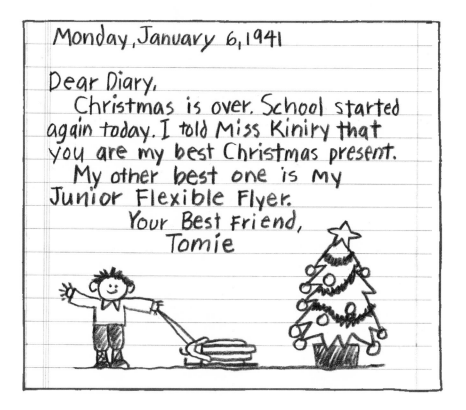

Monday, January 6, 1941

Dear Diary,
    Christmas is over. School started again today. I told Miss Kiniry that you are my best Christmas present.
    My other best one is my Junior Flexible Flyer.
            Your Best Friend,
                Tomie

I love writing in my diary. I can put my secret thoughts in it, and NO ONE will ever see them. Just in case, I always lock it and wear the key around my neck, even when I take a bath or go to sleep.

Christmas was really great this year. Santa left us a load of presents. I didn't get a wood-burning set, though. It was only the second time he had come to our house at 26 Fairmount Avenue in Meriden, Connecticut.

I love my Junior Flexible Flyer. Flexible Flyers are the best sleds ever made. (I wanted the big one, but I guess Santa thought the Senior was too heavy for me to pull back up the hill after I slid down it.)

When I woke up the day after Christmas, it had snowed. I raced downstairs. Dad was eating breakfast. Mom was reading the paper.

"Dad! Dad! Can we go sliding? Please, please? I have to try out my Junior Flexible Flyer."

"Okay, Tomie. Just let me finish my coffee, and we'll go," Dad said.

"Don't forget your hat and gloves," Mom called after me as I ran upstairs to get dressed. "And put on an extra pair of socks so your feet won't get cold!"

Dad and I headed over to the big empty lot

between Highland Avenue, Columbus Avenue, and Grove Road. I can't remember who owned it, but I think it was the Del Favaros. Anyway, it was VERY steep and fast.

Some grown-ups and kids were already there packing down the new snow. The hill had three sliding runs. One was for the older kids, like Buddy. It had bumps that would send the sled flying. If you were a younger kid, you could only go on it if you went on a sled with a grown-up or an older kid. The run for us younger kids was good and long, and the sled went pretty fast. The baby run was short and almost flat—just right for little kids.

When all the snow was packed down, we pulled our sleds up the hill and got in line. Finally it was my turn. I got on my sled. Dad gave me a push. Wow! I flew down that hill really fast, and I didn't fall off. My Junior Flexible Flyer was great!

From then on I was there every afternoon and even some early nights. On Saturdays, I'd spend practically the whole day sliding. I only went home for lunch. I'd stick my Junior Flexible Flyer into the snowbank the grown-ups made so we could "park" our sleds. Mom had hot cream of tomato soup and a grilled cheese sandwich waiting for me. Mom would make me change my two pairs of socks for dry ones and "warm up" before I could go back.

On Saturday afternoons, the older kids made "rippers." They tied lots of sleds together in one long line. They put the ropes they pulled the sleds with over the seat of the sled in front. This kept all the sleds together. The driver of the first sled was the one in control. If a younger kid was lucky—and I was—you could hitch a ride sitting up in front of an older kid or a grown-up.

I thought about kids who didn't have any snow in the winter. It's a good thing they didn't know how much fun they were missing, like tipping over on the "ripper" into the soft snow. Everyone would sit up, covered in snow, laughing and spitting out the white stuff.

One Saturday, it was getting dark, and we knew it was time to head home. We did one last "ripper" down the hill. Whoops! Over we went!

Buddy and I came in looking like snowmen.

"What happened to you two?" Mom asked. She was feeding our baby sister, Maureen.

"The 'ripper' tipped over," I said. "No one was hurt, just covered with snow."

"That's good," Mom said. "Go and get out of those wet things. As soon as your dad gets home, we'll eat."

When we sat down for supper, Mom said, "One of these nights, I'm going to tell you all about the Giant Ripper we had in Wallingford when I was a little girl. There was a terrible accident, and no one has ever forgotten it!"

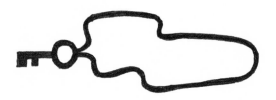

Chapter Two

Saturday, January 11, 1941

Dear Diary,
   Tonight after supper, Mom told us a really exciting and scary story. I love Mom's stories about when she was a little girl because they are true. Dad tells good stories, too. So does Tom! I think h e makes up some of them, though.
            Your best friend,
                Tomie

"It was winter when I was about nine or ten years old," Mom started. "There was so much snow that year that the town of Wallingford decided to block off some of the steeper streets so everyone could go sliding.

There weren't many cars in those days. The snow on the streets was packed down instead of being plowed. So it was perfect for winter fun.

"Don't forget, we didn't have radios then, so everyone, young people and grown-ups, all went sliding. But our sleds were different from yours. You couldn't 'steer' them the way you boys can steer your Flexible Flyers. You just got on your sled and went.

"Well, someone got the idea that it would be exciting to try a toboggan on the hill down Franklin Street. Lots of people could fit on a toboggan, and they thought it was safe because a toboggan doesn't have any runners, so it doesn't go very fast. In fact, it is just plain slow. Then somebody got the bright idea of making something like a toboggan and tying it on top of a bunch of sleds. They called it 'THE RIPPER' because of the way it 'ripped' down the hill with a whole lot of people on it, mostly grown-ups.

"Some parents thought it was too dangerous for kids. My mother, your grandmother

Nana Downstairs, was one of those parents. So, I had to stand and watch while all the people who were lucky enough to ride on 'The Ripper' zoomed down Franklin Street, yelling and screaming.

"Well, late one Sunday afternoon, my best friend, Edna Wood, came over and said she was going on 'The Ripper' and could I go, too.

"My mother said, 'NO!'

"Then Edna's father, Mr. Wood, came to the door and said, 'Mrs. Downey, Flossie will be fine. I'll be in the front with Edna and Flossie, and we've worked out a way to steer with ropes.'

"'I'll go with them,' Cousin Kitty, my mother's cousin from Brooklyn, who was visiting us, said.

"My mother broke down and said, 'Well, all right. But only ONE ride, Florence, NO MORE!'

"Cousin Kitty put on her long fur coat and her big fur hat, and off we went, with Cousin Kitty looking like a European queen.

"There was a crowd of people waiting at the top of Franklin Street. Everyone, including Cousin Kitty, piled onto 'The Ripper,' sitting in front and behind one another and holding on to legs and waists for the thrilling ride down the steep street.

"Mr. Wood was up front with Edna in his lap because he was doing the steering. I was right in front of them.

"Your Uncle Charles, my little brother, was standing watching. 'I'm gonna tell Ma that you were in front, and you're gonna get it!' he yelled.

"'Okay, Flossie,' Mr. Wood said, 'change places with Edna.' So I did.

"'ONE, TWO, THREE,' the crowd of men shouted, and they gave 'The Ripper' a big push. The snow was packed down so hard, it was almost like ice. Down the hill we flew, the air whizzing past us so fast, it took our breaths away. I clung to Edna, and Mr. Wood clung to both of us. Everyone was yelling and screaming! People up and down the street were cheering!

"All of a sudden, the blade of the front sled hit a stone or something. 'The Ripper' went out of control, and Mr. Wood couldn't steer it. 'The Ripper' hit a tree, and people went flying everywhere.

"I was knocked out. When I came to, people were running around and shouting. Some lay on the snowbanks with broken bones. Lots of people had nosebleeds. It was AWFUL!

"Edna had a huge cut on her face and lip. Mr. Wood had hit the tree with the side of his face. They were taken off to the doctor's office with lots of other people. I couldn't see Cousin Kitty anywhere.

"I had a huge bump on my head, and it was getting bigger all the time. I was crying and trying to run home. Charles found me. He had my hat in his hand. He put it on my head and ran along with me, shouting, 'Ma,

Pa, come help. Flossie's brains are coming out!'

"When we got to the house, my mother asked, 'Oh my goodness, what happened?'

"Charles told her.

"My father, your grandfather, Tom, got a big chunk of ice out of the icebox and put it on my head.

"'Well, young lady,' my mother said, 'that's the last time I change my mind about something you want to do! Where's Kitty? Was she on "The Ripper," too?'

"Just then the doorbell rang. Two neighbors were holding Cousin Kitty between them. She looked a mess. Her furs were wet from the snow, and one of her eyes was all red. 'That's going to be the biggest shiner I've ever seen,' my father said.

"Mother helped Cousin Kitty upstairs while the men told my father all about the accident.

"'Nothing like this has ever happened in Wallingford,' one of the men said. 'Thank God no one was killed.' That was true, but lots of people were seriously hurt. My friend Edna had a scar on her face for the rest of her life.

"Cousin Kitty stayed with us for several more weeks—until her black eye went away. 'I'm not going back to Brooklyn looking like this,' she said.

"Needless to say," Mom finished, "that was the end of the famous Wallingford 'Ripper.'"

Chapter Three

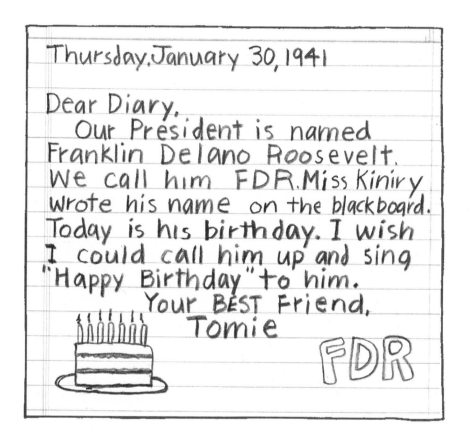

Thursday. January 30, 1941

Dear Diary,
    Our President is named Franklin Delano Roosevelt. We call him FDR. Miss Kiniry wrote his name on the blackboard. Today is his birthday. I wish I could call him up and sing "Happy Birthday" to him.
            Your BEST Friend,
                Tomie

FDR

January was the month of the March of Dimes. Before he was president, FDR caught this terrible disease called "infantile paralysis." It was also called "polio."

Lots of children caught polio, too. Some of them ended up not being able to walk without crutches or metal braces on their legs. The worst thing about polio is that sometimes you can't breathe by yourself, so you have to be put in a big metal thing called an "iron lung." Mom told me that the iron lung "breathes" for the person inside. I think that's scary.

Because President Roosevelt's birthday was at the end of January, practically the whole month was spent trying to raise money to stop polio. Mr. Eddy Cantor, who sang on the radio and made movies, said we should call the event the March of Dimes after the short subject movie called the *March of Time*. "All those dimes marching to find a cure," he said.

I guess because a dime isn't that much money, even kids could help. Each classroom had a chart on the blackboard. All of us

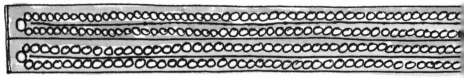

kids went around to houses in our neighbor-hoods to collect dimes.

The radio station WTIC, in Hartford, the state capital of Connecticut, had a thing they called the "Mile of Dimes." Uncle Charles took Buddy and me up to see it. It was a long, long red thing that looked like a table with slots running the whole length. The slots were a mile long and just wide enough for dimes. Every year WTIC tried to collect more dimes than they collected the year before.

People brought the dimes in bags and put them in the mile-long slots. WTIC inter-viewed some of the people on the radio.

"And who do we have here?" the announcer would say.

"I'm 'so-and-so' from Bristol, Bob," the person would say.

"That looks like quite a few bags full of dimes you have there. How much are you bringing?"

"We collected from the third-floor work-
ers of the Waltham Watch Factory, and I'm
proud to say we raised over three hundred
dollars."

The people watching would clap.

"Maybe you boys can bring your dimes
here next year," Uncle Charles said. "You
could be on the radio!"

"Really?" I said. I started making plans in
my head.

"I'm not going to be on any radio," Buddy
said.

Older brothers!

The March of Dimes ended with a ball in
Washington, D.C. (That's a big dance where
everyone gets dressed up.) President and
Mrs. Roosevelt would be there to thank
everyone! They would be broadcast on the
radio along with the dance music.

Mom said she'd love Dad to take her some year. Me, too, I thought. I'd love to meet President Roosevelt. He had a Scottie dog named Fala. I thought it was great that our president had a Scottie. Dad had met President Roosevelt when he was running for president the second time. Dad didn't meet Fala, though.

Every year for the March of Dimes, my favorite radio program, "Let's Pretend," acted out the story of *The Little Lame Prince* in honor of the president's birthday.

I liked listening to the play on the radio a lot, but I really wanted to read the book. The library had it, but it was in the third-grade section where longer books were. I was only allowed to take out books from the FIRST-grade section. If I couldn't read harder books, how could I learn more and more words? I don't know who made up that "rule," but I thought it was stupid!

Chapter Four

> Friday, February 14, 1941
>
> Dear Diary,
>   Today was Valentine's Day. They used the Valentine mailbox I made last year for the First Grade and Kindergarten. I got lots of Valentines.
>   Roses are red, Violets are blue,
> I've got a Diary and it is YOU!
>   Hearts and Flowers
>   Y.B.F.I.T.W.
>   ♡Tomie

Sometimes on Saturday mornings we went to the movies just for kids. Buddy took me and my best friend, Jeannie Houdlette. Sometimes Carol Crane came, too. (He didn't like taking us much.) All three movie theaters, the Palace, the Capitol, and the old Loew's Poli, had special Saturday morning kiddie shows. Before the long movie started, they had a short movie called a "serial." It was like watching one chapter of an exciting adventure story. Usually the hero or the heroine was in terrible danger at the end of each one. You had to come back the next week to find out what happened.

Mom told me that when she was a little girl, one serial ran for fifteen weeks. She and her father, my grandfather, Tom, went every week for fourteen weeks. They were really excited about seeing the ending. But, guess what. They TORE the movie theater down. They never did find out how the serial ended!

The first movie stars I ever liked were Shirley Temple, of course, and the famous movie star Miss Mae West. My mother used to take me with her to movies before I started school. That's how I knew Miss Mae West. But Miss West wasn't making as many movies as she had before. Something about her being "too RISKAY," my mom told me.

My two new favorite movie stars were teenagers! They sang and danced and were always putting on shows to feed the orphans or to send the city kids to the country for the summer. Their names were Mickey Rooney and Judy Garland. Judy Garland was in *The Wizard of Oz* when she was younger. She sang "Over the Rainbow."

Miss Leah, my dancing teacher, said, "You know, Tommy, I'll bet you can be as good as Mickey Rooney. We'll just have to find you a 'Judy'!" (I was Tommy at dancing school, too! Just like at school!)

Today, Mom was taking Jeannie, Carol Crane, and me to see *Fantasia*. It was Mr. Walt Disney's new movie. (Buddy was going to another theater to see a cowboy movie.) Mom said *Fantasia* didn't have a story like *Snow White* or *Pinocchio*. So I knew it was going to be different from his other movies. But I didn't know how.

It was a real surprise. It had classical music. That's music that an orchestra plays and grown-ups go to concerts to listen to.

Kids go, too. But what was different was that Mr. Walt Disney showed different pictures on the screen that seemed to go with the music that was playing—happy, sad, exciting, strange—all kinds of music. But no talking! Except when a Master of Ceremonies introduced each piece of music.

Some of the scenes were really beautiful, like the "Nutcracker Suite." I liked the way milkweed seeds became ballerinas floating down onto a brook. I also liked the Chinese dance. The dancers were mushrooms!

Then there was Mickey Mouse as the Sorcerer's Apprentice. He had to carry buckets of water from the well, up the stairs to the sorcerer's magic chamber. But Mickey got tired, so he found a spell in the sorcerer's book and enchanted the broom to carry the water. But he couldn't stop it! The whole place flooded. What a disaster. Finally, the sorcerer came home, saw what was happening, and put a stop to it. Everyone liked that part!

There was another part with very strange music. It didn't seem to have any tune, just drums beating. The pictures were about the beginning of the earth when dinosaurs lived there. It was VERY exciting.

A really funny one was called "Dance of the Hours." Elephants, hippopotamuses, ostriches, and crocodiles did all the dancing. It was very silly. I laughed a lot.

It was such an interesting movie with so many things to see. I wondered where Mr. Walt Disney got his ideas.

When I got home, I couldn't stop talking about it. Mom said maybe I could see it again. I liked seeing favorite movies more than once. I missed so much the first time.

Sunday, March 9, 1941

Dear Diary,
   Today is Mom's birthday. She gave Buddy, Maureen and me a present at breakfast! Mom always gives us a present on HER BIRTHDAY. I am giving Mom a pretty lace handkerchief with an F for Florence. (But Mom likes to be called Floss or Flossie.)
               Y. B. F. I. T. W.
                    Tomie

Saturday, March 15, 1941

Dear Diary.
   Two kids in our class have SCARLET FEVER! It is terrible! You have to stay in a dark room. It is so catchy, they burn all your books and clothes and TOYS!!! No one can see you. They put a sign on your house that says "Quarantine." (I copied it from the Meahs' front door.) It means stay away or else! I hope I don't get IT! Gee, Diary, it isn't easy being a kid. Y.B.F.I.T.W.-still alive,
               Tomie

Tuesday, March 25, 1941

Dear Diary,
    Tomorrow is Maureen's birthday.
She is one year old! Mom is having
a party for her.
            Y. B. F. I. T. W.
                Tomie

Tuesday, April 1, 1941

Dear Diary,

    I HATE YOU!!!!

APRIL FOOLS! HA-HA-HA-HA-HA!
    I love you, Dear Diary.
            Y. B. F. I. T. W.
                Tomie

Chapter Five

Thursday, April 10, 1941

Dear Diary,
    Sunday is Easter. We are going to Nana Fall-River's house. I hope the Easter Bunny finds us.
        Happy Easter!
        Y. B. F. I. T. W.
            Tomie

I don't know whose idea it was to go to Nana Fall-River's house for Easter. Nana lives in Fall River, Massachusetts, along with some of our other Italian relatives. It is a long, long car ride—about three days—only kidding! But it is three hours, and I get carsick.

Plain, unbuttered popcorn helps keep me

from throwing up. So after the car was packed, the first stop was Alexander's Karmel Krisp Kandy Shop to get a couple of bags of plain, plain popcorn! I had to eat it slowly so it would last—one kernel at a time.

Buddy sat up front with Dad. Mom, Maureen, and I sat in the back. I liked that a lot. Mom played all kinds of games with us.

"Look, Tomie," Mom said. "Burma Shave signs." They were my favorite signs. A shave cream company put signs up along the highways. There would be one sign after another with a few words on each one. Mom read the signs out loud as we drove along. They were in rhyme like a poem and really funny, like this one.

DON'T STICK YOUR ELBOW	OUT SO FAR	IT MIGHT GO HOME	IN ANOTHER CAR

And the last sign—

BURMA SHAVE

When we arrived at Nana Fall-River's house, everyone wanted to see Maureen. Uncle Frank, my dad's oldest brother, his wife, Aunt Susie, and their daughters, Cousin Frances and Cousin Connie, came down from upstairs where they lived. And Dad's youngest sister, Aunt Clorinda, and her husband, Uncle Billy, came over with their little boy, Paul. This was the first time Mom had brought Maureen to visit, so she was the center of attention.

The biggest room in Nana's house was the dining room. It was also the kitchen. Nana cooked all the time. That's where the family all sat around the big table, talking and eating. They'd talk and talk, and sit and sit, and eat and eat. (Nana had a parlor with a big sofa and uncomfortable chairs, but everyone always sat around the table.)

Just like always, we kids had to sit there and be quiet. Finally, Mom gave me a little nod. I slid off my chair and went upstairs to Uncle Frank's. Aunt Susie wasn't Italian, so she had stuff to eat, like jelly doughnuts, that I liked better than Nana's Italian food. And they had a piano. "Tomie," my cousin Frances said, "come here and I'll teach you to play 'Chopsticks.'"

Later Mom called me downstairs for supper.

We had spaghetti with no meatballs. That's because it was Good Friday, and Good Friday is very strict about no meat. I have to say that kids never got meatballs at Nana Fall-River's house. Only the grown-ups *always* did. But on Good Friday no one, grown-ups or kids, even got tomato sauce on the spaghetti!

On Easter Sunday when
I woke up, I found small
Easter baskets of candy
and a stuffed toy for
Maureen and me from
the Easter Bunny. (Buddy
was too old to get any!)

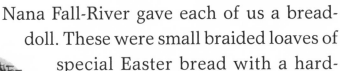

Nana Fall-River gave each of us a bread-
doll. These were small braided loaves of
special Easter bread with a hard-
boiled egg in it like a little face.
Nana made them every year for
all her grandchildren, no matter
how old they were.

After church Nana Fall-River
began to get ready to cook Easter
dinner. The saying at Nana Fall-
River's house was that when the church bell
rang twelve times, Nana would put the water
for the "Macaron" on the stove and dinner
would be ready at 12:18. It was true.

Before noon other relatives began to
arrive for dinner. The table was all set with a
nice tablecloth on the big table. (Nana Fall-

River's table was much bigger than Tom and Nana's in Wallingford.) The only thing that I thought was funny, was that before the food was put down, Nana Fall-River spread out newspapers in the center of the table—to keep the nice tablecloth clean, I guess.

"Come on, Tomie," Dad said. "We're going across the street to Marzilli's Bakery to get fresh bread." I loved Marzilli's Bakery. It smelled so good, and there was this HUGE oven made out of bricks with a real fire in it.

Nana cut the bread and put it in a huge tower in the middle of the table. Everyone sat down, eating, talking, eating, more talking, more eating, for what seemed like hours.

Plates were changed, more bread was cut. Finally the Easter cheese pies were brought to the table along with a big bowl of fruit.

"Well, what do you all think about the fighting that's going on in Europe?" Uncle Frank asked.

"I don't think that the Italians should get mixed up in it," Aunt Clorinda said.

"They already are," Uncle Billy said.

"*Basta*. Enough," Nana Fall-River said loudly. She said some more in Italian. Everyone stopped talking English.

"What are they talking about?" I whispered to Buddy.

"None of your business," Buddy answered. "You're too young to understand."

"Okay, boys," Mom said. "You're excused. Grab some cookies and go outside. Only one, Tomie."

Buddy and I went outside. I had to be careful about what I ate because

34

we were going to head home later that afternoon. And no one wanted me to get carsick
and throw up. But I "snuck" a couple of
marshmallow chicks from my Easter basket
to eat anyhow.

"Good-bye, good-bye—*arrivederci*," the
relatives called as we drove off, the car
packed with food from Nana Fall-River. It
began to get dark. Maureen and I fell asleep.

"Wake up, Tomie," Mom said to me. "We're
here. And good job! You didn't get carsick!"

I was glad to be home at 26 Fairmount
Avenue.

Chapter Six

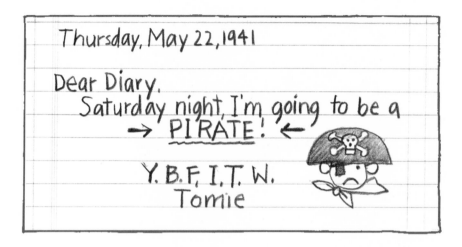

Thursday, May 22, 1941

Dear Diary,
    Saturday night, I'm going to be a
      → PIRATE! ←

        Y. B. F, I. T. W.
         Tomie

This was my second year at "Miss Leah Grossman's School of Dance." There were lots of new kids this year. They were lucky because Miss Leah was the best dance teacher in the world. Her recitals were just like going to the movies to see all those movie stars singing and dancing. Why, even people who didn't have children in the dancing school came!

The second year tap class was four girls and me. We were going to be a band of pirates in the Spring Recital. I was the only boy, so I would be the leader. Our number was called "Ali Baba and the Pirates."

I looked at pictures of pirates in books to see what we might look like.

Pirates are really gruesome. Maybe I'd get to wear a hook on my hand or a wooden peg leg or a black patch over my eye.

Then Miss Leah showed us the costume sketches that always came from New York City. No hooks, no peg legs, no eye patches. Oh, well! At least we would wear big boots, and hats with a skull and crossbones on them! And we would have these fake swords called SCIMITARS!

Our hats and boots and my shorts and the girls' skirts would be made out of black oil-cloth, which was very shiny—and very stiff. Our boots weren't really boots. They fit over our tap shoes and had big, big cuffs on them. Our shirts and my shorts and the girls' skirts had jagged edges on the bottoms and the sleeves. We would all wear bright colored sashes where our scimitars hung. And we would have pirate hats with a skull and crossbones on them.

I knew I couldn't have a hook or a peg leg, but it wasn't too soon to start asking if I could at least have a patch over my eye so I'd look scary. I started by giving Miss Leah drawings of pirates. Every one of them had an eye patch. Miss Leah got what I was trying to tell her.

One Saturday, she said to me, "Okay, Tommy, you can have an eye patch, but *not* the girls."

"How about holding my scimitar in my mouth while I dance?" I suggested.

Miss Leah said, "I think the eye patch will be quite enough!"

It was the BIG night! The audience was waiting. Mom, Dad, Buddy, Nana, Uncle Charles and his girlfriend, Viva, and Tom were there. Our pirate band was dressed up and ready.

I opened our number on the stage by myself with a song called "I Ain't Afraid of a Policeman." I guess Miss Leah thought it would be "cute" for a little pirate to sing a song that ended: "I ain't afraid of a policeman, 'cuz he's just another man like Dad."

The audience clapped and clapped.

Then my pirate band came on stage. They clapped some more.

I danced out in front. I was the shortest, so I didn't hide the two tall girls in the middle of the line.

I waved my scimitar around in the air as if I was showing my pirates how to do it. The girls pretended to bang their scimitars

against one another. They made a noise with
their taps to make it sound like the swords
hitting together.

The audience loved our number.

It was a very good recital, except I was a
little sorry I hadn't done a "specialty" number like I did last year with Joan Ciotti when
we danced as "The Farmer in the Dell and
His Wife."

After the recital, all the kids dressed up in their best clothes to dance with a real orchestra. We'd never done that before after a recital!

Miss Leah came out in the evening dress she wore for our finale. I wasn't very shy, so I asked Mom and Dad if I could ask Miss Leah for a dance. They smiled and said, "Sure!" I was going to ask Jean Minor and Patty Clark, too.

Miss Leah was talking with a man, so I waited. I heard him say, "You know, Leah, I missed that little dePaola kid doing another dance number. He's really got talent. Next year, you should give him a specialty."

"With so many students this year, we just didn't have time," Miss Leah said. "But that's a good idea for next year."

WOW!!! I didn't know whether I could wait a WHOLE year or not! I guess I'd just have to.

When Miss Leah and I started to do a two-step, all the people stopped dancing to watch us. Little, short ME dancing with my tall, glamorous dancing teacher! It was wonderful! I forgot all about not doing a specialty number in the recital. I was doing it right NOW! Maybe Miss Leah would be my "Judy."

Tuesday, May 27, 1941

Dear Diary,
    Mom took me to the library
after school. I can still only take
ONE book from the First Grade
shelf. Oh well! Wait until September.
            Y. B. F. I. T. W.
            Tomie

ONLY ONE BOOK
BOO!

Friday, May 30, 1941

Dear Diary,
    We took flowers to school
today. They will decorate the
graves of soldiers who did all the
fighting in wars. We call it
Decoration Day because of the
flowers. The real name is Memorial
Day. Miss Kiniry says that memorial
means to remember.
        See you, Dear Diary.
            Y. B. F. I. T. W.
                Tomie

Saturday, July 5, 1941

Dear Diary,
   Well, I ate too many hot dogs
and I threw up. I missed all
the July 4th fireworks. So I
can't tell you anything about them.
         Your GREEN friend,
         Y. B. F. I. T. W.
            Tomie

Sunday, July 27, 1941

Dear Diary,
      We can't go swimming!
We can't go to the movies. We
can't go anywhere! Mom says there's
some polio in Connecticut. I sure
don't want to catch it like F.D.R.
did. It is really boring right now.
      I wish school would start. I
wonder who my new teacher will
be?   Your "I'm going crazy" friend.
         Y. B. F. I. T. W.
            Tomie   ? ? ?

Chapter Seven

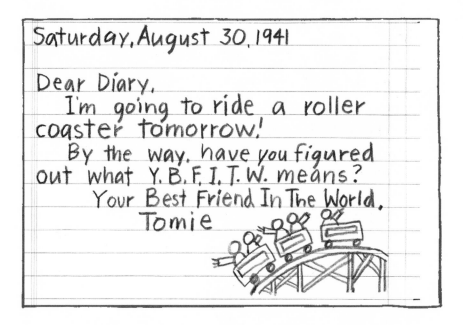

Saturday, August 30, 1941

Dear Diary,
    I'm going to ride a roller coaster tomorrow!
    By the way, have you figured out what Y. B. F. I. T. W. means?
        Your Best Friend In The World,
            Tomie

Every summer Dad and Mom took us to the amusement park. It was called Savin Rock. My grandfather, Tom, came, too! We went today because it was Buddy's birthday.

Savin Rock was an amusement park outside of New Haven, Connecticut. It was on the shoreline of Long Island Sound and had lots of rides and games and food. There was a big roller coaster that went over the water, a Fun

House that you walked through, and a merry-go-round, of course. In fact, they had two—a grown-up one where all the animals went up and down, and one for little kids where the animals didn't move.

After we parked the car, I asked Tom to come and watch a ride I wouldn't be allowed to go on "until you're in high school," Mom said. It was called the Virginia Reel. Tom and I stood by the fence and watched the cars that looked like big tubs go up a big hill on the track. At the top the car let go, and twirled around and zigzagged down the track going faster and faster and changing direction at each turn. The people, especially the ladies, screamed and looked very frightened. They seemed very glad when the ride was over.

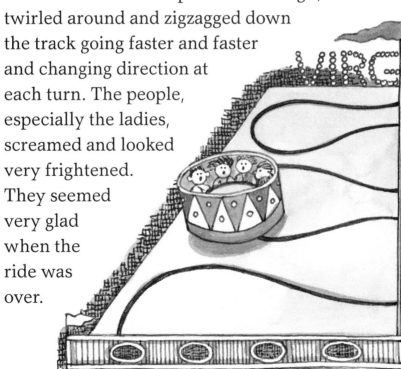

"One of the kids told me that people got thrown out of one of the cars once," I told Tom. "They said that about the big roller coaster, too!"

"Well," said Tom, "I don't think that's true. They're still running, aren't they? If they were *that* dangerous, the city would have closed them down."

One of the great places was the Penny Arcade. It was a big, big building with all kinds of games in it.

You could watch "movies" by putting in a penny and turning a crank. They were VERY old-fashioned, and there were some that said "NO CHILDREN—ADULTS ONLY." Tom told me that they were "movies" of fat ladies dancing!

There was a shooting gallery and all kinds of ring toss and bowling games. I won a candy bowl for Nana.

We always went to the cotton candy stand. I loved to watch the man make the cotton candy, twirling the paper cone and filling it up with pink sugary candy. Cotton candy melted in your mouth. If you tried to bite it off the cone, it got all over your face. The best way to eat it was to pick pieces off and plop them in your mouth.

Tom took me on the "Laff in the Dark" ride. We got in the car and pulled a safety bar down over our laps. Then the car started down the track. It banged open a door and in we went! It was pitch black. We heard all this creepy laughing all around us.

"Tom, Tom," I cried, "there're cobwebs in my hair!"

"I don't feel anything," Tom said.

"You have your cap on," I said.

"Watch out!" Tom yelled. Things jumped out at us—skeletons, green faces, witches. I screamed! I was glad Tom was with me. The car twisted and turned in the dark. Finally, we banged through another door, and we were out in the daylight again!

"Safe and sound," Tom said with a smile.

As we were getting ready to leave the Penny Arcade, we saw a booth with a sign: "Make Your Own Records." "Well," Tom said. "Let's give Cousin Morton a run for his money."

Tom and I went into a little room with a glass window in it and a microphone hanging from the ceiling. "Okay," the man outside said. He had all his equipment in front of him. His voice came over a speaker. "Count to ten. You first, Grandpa! Great. Now you, little boy. I'll give you a count of three and you start."

Tom introduced us, and he sang "I Went to the Animal Farm," then I sang my recital song, "I Ain't Afraid of a Policeman."

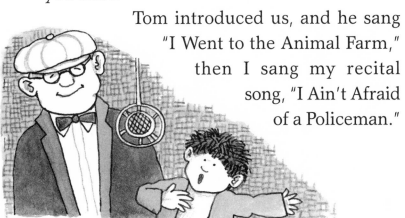

When we finished, the man said we were terrific and how would we like to hear the record. Well, he played it over a loudspeaker, and a lot of people gathered around to listen. When the record was over, the people clapped! "Maybe we could send it to Cousin Morton, and maybe he'll play it on the radio!" I said to Tom. Tom laughed.

Outside, I saw the Kiddie Koaster. It was a little roller coaster for little kids. I wanted to go on it. Mom said I was too young to go by myself, and Buddy wouldn't go on it with me! "That's for BABIES!" he said.

"I'll go," Tom said. So, Tom squeezed himself in the little car. His knees were way up to his ears. People watching laughed and pointed. "Atta way, Grandpa!" they yelled.

"C'mon, Tomie," Tom said after he squeezed out of the roller coaster car. "Time for the giant Ferris wheel!" It was higher than the kiddie one. We went up so high, we could see all over the amusement park and out into Long Island Sound. The Ferris wheel stopped with our car at the top. It swayed a little back and forth. I felt very safe with Tom's arm around me. "Wait until you tell your friend Jeannie about this!" Tom said.

We had hot dogs and caramel corn and drinks.

Finally, as it was getting dark and all the lights started coming on all over the park, we went into the Wax Museum. Outside it said it was "Highly Educational." I thought it was just plain creepy. Rooms filled with dusty wax dummies.

Before we left the park, Buddy got to go on the bumper cars with Dad. I had to wait until I was nine. There was a sign that said "No One Under Nine Years of Age."

We headed home. We dropped Tom off in Wallingford, at his and Nana's house, and picked up Maureen.

I wrote in my diary a little bit and fell fast asleep. After all, the next day was the Labor Day picnic. School was going to start Wednesday! And MY birthday was coming soon!

Chapter Eight

Wednesday, September 3, 1941

Dear Diary,
    School started today! Hooray
for second grade! I can't wait for
ART lessons to start!
        Your SECOND GRADE friend,
            Tomie

School at last! We went to Miss Kiniry's
room and waited. Finally Miss Philomena
came in and told us what second-grade room
we'd be in. I was in Miss Gardner's room. So
was Jeannie Houdlette and lots of my friends.

I went to Miss Gardner's room and looked
around. I didn't see any fall leaves decorat-
ing the walls like some of the other rooms.

Instead I saw lots of ARITHMETIC charts up—all numbers. Maybe I'd tell Miss Gardner that I could do some pictures for the bulletin board.

Second grade was NOT like first grade. About a week after school started, it was my birthday. On September 15 I was seven years old. Last year Miss Kiniry let Mom come to the class on my birthday with a sheet cake for everyone. But Miss Gardner didn't allow birthdays in class, so no cake or cookies at school.

Instead Mom said that I could pick out four friends, and she would take us to the Wild Animal Farm in Southington after school.

When we got there, we saw a crow at the place where you went in. The man said the crow could talk, but it sounded just like "caw-caw" to me.

Inside we saw bunnies, a fox, a beaver, weasels, peacocks—but no tigers or boa constrictors like I hoped we would. But we had fun anyhow.

I got some great presents this year—a wood-burning set, a pair of ball-bearing roller skates (now I'm wearing two keys around my neck—my diary key and my skate key) and best of all, a box of 64 CRAYOLA crayons.

I knew we were going to have real art lessons this year with Mrs. Bowers, the real art teacher. I had already met Mrs. Bowers once when I was in kindergarten and made the valentine mailbox. Mrs. Bowers saw it and told me how much she really liked it. I wished Mrs. Bowers would hurry up and get here.

I took my crayons to school the next day. I wanted to be ready for Mrs. Bowers whenever she finally came.

Miss Gardner saw them and said, "Tommy, take those crayons home and leave them there."

Miss Gardner wanted us all to use the same stupid school crayons. She only gave us one piece of paper, too!

Mom told me that Mrs. Bowers only came to the school every two months or so. And she had to go to all the classrooms, not just ours.

But finally, one afternoon before we went home, Miss Gardner told us that Mrs. Bowers was coming to our classroom the next day.

Well, that night I could hardly sleep.

The next morning, Mrs. Bowers came in wearing her blue artist's smock and carrying a big box of thick colored chalks. (I had secretly brought my 64 Crayolas to school even though Miss Gardner had "forbidden" them in her classroom. When I saw those colored chalks, I was sure Mrs. Bowers would understand.)

Two boys from sixth grade followed her into the classroom, holding a big, big piece of paper from the paper roll at the end of the hallway.

Mrs. Bowers put the paper up over the blackboard. She turned around, and I knew the ART LESSON was about to begin. I wasn't sure what it would be, but I was excited and ready.

Well, the morning started off badly. First of all, Miss Gardner handed out those AWFUL school crayons and our ONE piece of paper.

Then Mrs. Bowers started to talk about Thanksgiving coming, and how we would learn to draw a Pilgrim man, a Pilgrim lady, and a turkey.

Oh, boy, I thought. *This will help me when I make the place cards for Thanksgiving dinner!*

"So now, boys and girls," Mrs. Bowers said, "copy what I do!"

Copy? Real artists don't copy. My twin cousins told me that. They should know because they had studied at a real art school in Brooklyn.

I just sat there. Miss Gardner saw me sitting with a frown on my face. She said something to Mrs. Bowers. They came over to my desk.

"What's the matter now?" Miss Gardner asked.

I didn't answer. I took my 64 Crayolas out of my desk and spoke to Mrs. Bowers. I told her about the one piece of paper. I told her about my cousins and how real artists don't copy.

"And besides," I said, "I am going to be an ARTIST when I grow up."

Then I told Mrs. Bowers how I had drawn right on my sheets, under the covers, and how Mom and Dad had let me draw on the walls before they put on the plaster when they were building our new house. I told her I drew whenever I could!

Well, was I lucky. Mrs. Beulah Bowers understood completely.

"But I have to be fair to the rest of the children, Tommy," she said. "So if you draw the Pilgrims and the turkey using the school crayons, I'll give you another piece of paper, and you can draw whatever you want with your own crayons."

"Okay," I said, and I did. I changed the way Mrs. Bowers drew noses, though. I liked the way I drew them better. I think she did, too!

For my own drawing, I drew a picture of Mrs. Bowers in her blue smock and with all the beautiful combs in her hair. She asked if she could have it, but I explained that I had to keep it. She understood that, too.

That day Mrs. Bowers and I became really GOOD friends. She never came to our school without saying, "Hello, Tommy. Do any new drawings lately?"

Mrs. Bowers knew the answer would be yes, and she always took the time for me to show them to her.

Halloween, Friday, October 31, 1941

Dear Diary,
    Wow! I got lots of candy tonight!
I went out dressed as a Rich Lady.
I wore Mom's fur and jewelry.
Just like Cousin Kitty. No one
knew me!
            Your best friend,
            Tomie, the Artist

Saturday, November 15, 1941

Dear Diary,
    Well, I finally have my "Judy."
There are only four of us in class
at Miss Leah's, Patty Clark, Billy Burns,
and Carol Morrissey! She is my
partner. I think she is even better
than Joan Ciotti.
        Watch out, Mickey and Judy!
            Your best friend,
            Tomie

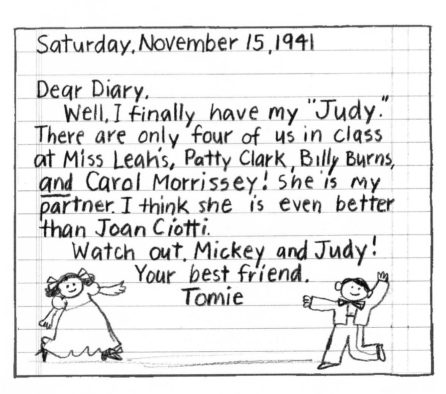

Sunday, November 30, 1941

Dear Diary,
    I made the place cards for Thanksgiving Dinner! I drew Pilgrim Ladies for Nana and Mom. I drew Pilgrim Men for Tom, Dad and Uncle Charles. I drew Pilgrim Boys for Buddy and me. I drew a Pilgrim Baby for Maureen.
    Nana liked them.
    Christmas is coming fast. We saw Santa Claus turn the lights on downtown. I need to make my Christmas lists!!
            Your Best Friend,
            Tomie

Chapter Nine

Sunday, December 7, 1941

Dear Diary,
   A lot happened today.
I'm not sure I understand it,
but I will never forget it.
      Your Best Friend,
         Tomie

Sundays were pretty much the same at 26 Fairmount Avenue. I'd get up kind of early to read the comics. We called them "the funnies." We got the *Sunday Herald Tribune*, the *Journal American* and the *New York Sunday Mirror*. They all had different "funnies."

Buddy liked the *Mirror* because it had "Dick Tracy" and "Joe Palooka." My favorite was the *Journal American*. "Jiggs and Maggie" (also called "Bringing Up Father") was on the front page, and the "Katzenjammer Kids" was on the back.

We'd turn on the radio and listen to Uncle Don read the comics as we followed along.

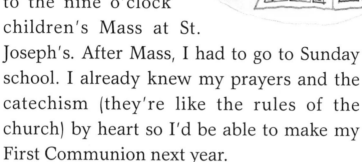

Then we all went to the nine o'clock children's Mass at St. Joseph's. After Mass, I had to go to Sunday school. I already knew my prayers and the catechism (they're like the rules of the church) by heart so I'd be able to make my First Communion next year.

When we got back home, I'd play outside or listen to the radio. I liked a show called the "Horn & Hardardt Children's Hour." It had children performers singing or playing musical instruments, things like that. . . .

Horn & Hardardt's was a chain of restaurants called AUTOMATS. A girl started each radio program singing the song—"Less work for mother, let's give her a hand."

I think they wanted families to take the mothers out to eat at the Horn & Hardardt's Automat.

Mom told me she'd been to one in New York City, where the show came from. She said that you looked through some little glass doors and picked out what you wanted to eat—maybe a sandwich, or a piece of pie or some cake. You put a dime in a slot and the little glass door opened. You took out whatever food you had picked. It sounded neat.

Then it was time for Sunday dinner, the biggest meal of the week. Most of the people I knew had a big Sunday dinner at noontime, like us. This Sunday, we were in the middle of eating. It was around one o'clock or maybe a little after. The phone rang. Mom answered it.

"What?" she said. "Joe, turn on the radio quick."

Dad got up and went into the living room to turn on the radio.

"We interrupt this program to bring you a news bulletin," the announcer said. "The Japanese air forces have just bombed Pearl Harbor."

Mom ran into the living room. The announcer went on talking. I didn't really understand.

"What's happening?" I asked Buddy.

"I don't know. I'm not sure," he answered.

The phone rang again. Mom answered it. "Oh, yes," she said. "Please come up. We need to be together."

Mom said that Nana, Tom, Uncle Charles, and his girlfriend, Viva, were on their way to our house.

Mom turned to Buddy and me. "Finish your dinner, boys. Then you can have some pie. We're not going to Wallingford today."

That was funny. We always went to Nana and Tom's on Sundays.

Mom and Dad stayed by the radio. Mom looked really worried. So did Dad. All I could figure out was that something awful had happened.

Tom, Nana, Uncle Charles, and Viva came in.

I went to Tom. "Can you read me the funnies?" I asked.

"Not right now, Timothy." (Tom called me
Timothy as a nickname.) "Maybe later."

The grown-ups all sat or stood around the
living room. Mom hadn't even cleared the
dishes from the table. The announcer kept
on talking. He got more and more excited.

Then I heard the words, "Our entire Pacific
Fleet has been destroyed. Thousands of men
and women have been killed." I wasn't sure
what a *fleet* was, but I knew what the word
destroyed meant. I knew what *killed* meant.

"This means WAR," Uncle Charles said. Viva started to cry. Mom, too! Even Nana dabbed at her eyes with her handkerchief.

"Are we going to be in the war?" Buddy asked.

"How come?" I whispered to Buddy.

No one said a word. I didn't know what was happening!

Mom picked up Maureen and hugged all three of us.

Dad hugged us, too.

"Oh, boys," Mom said through her tears. "Things will never be the same!"

The End
(And it was true. They wouldn't be.)